MUSIC THROUGHOUT HISTORY™

HANDEL'S WORLD

LAVINA LEE

rosen publishing's
rosen
central®

New York

For Wayne

Published in 2008 by The Rosen Publishing Group, Inc.
29 East 21st Street, New York, NY 10010

First Edition

Library of Congress Cataloging-in-Publication Data

Lee, Lavina.
Handel's world / Lavina Lee.—1st ed.
  p. cm.—(Music throughout history)
Includes bibliographical references (p.   ) and index.
ISBN-13: 978-1-4042-0726-4
ISBN-10: 1-4042-0726-0 (library binding)
1. Handel, George Frideric, 1685–1759. 2. Composers—
Biography. I. Title. II. Series.
ML410.H13L27 2006
780.92—dc22
                                                     2005030127

Manufactured in the United States of America

On the cover: Painting of George Frideric Handel by Jan
van der Banck.

CONTENTS

George Frideric Handel's dedication to his music made him a leading composer of the baroque movement. His most famous piece, *Messiah*, ensures his popularity, even today.

INTRODUCTION

Fewer than 100 years after the death of George Frideric Handel, Ludwig van Beethoven (1770–1827) described him as the greatest composer who ever lived. Such lofty praise from another great composer speaks much about Handel's influence on the musical world. This influence is obvious still.

Whether you know the name of the man who composed it, you have probably heard Handel's *Messiah*. The ubiquitous oratorio, perhaps best known by its "Hallelujah" chorus, has been performed every year since its premiere to a packed audience in Dublin, Ireland, in 1742. It has also become intertwined with the winter holidays, as it is now traditionally performed during Christmas celebrations in churches and concert halls worldwide.

Messiah, however, is not the only composition by Handel that is worth remembering. Its creation occupied only twenty-four of his thousands of music-composing days. Handel, known best for this famous oratorio and the majestic *Water Music*, was also a renowned organist and the composer of more than fifty operas, a musical form he tried desperately—and, for a while, quite successfully—to popularize in England.

In the early eighteenth century, when Handel began composing his own operas, the form had already been around for just over 100 years. Opera sparked the beginning of the baroque movement, which originated in Italy before spreading throughout Europe. In the baroque era, opera flourished with the use of single vocal lines and an emphasis on emotion. It was in England where Handel's career with this form would alternately flourish, struggle, and ultimately fizzle at the whim of the country's theatergoing audience.

Handel's time in England, his adoptive country, occupies the bulk of his life story. It was there that his name first became a household name, and where his musical contributions improved upon and made opera and, later, oratorio popular. The composer's story, though, begins not in England, where his extensive travels eventually took him. It begins in what is now Germany, where details about Handel's early life, including his family and his talent at playing the organ, take hazy shape. Even less information about his personal affairs or even his opinions exists.

A few things about Handel, however, can be gleaned from the various accounts about him. He had a quick temper and was known for having tense relationships with the actors and singers in his company. But, as musician Charles Burney observed, as quoted by biographer Christopher Hogwood, "Handel's general outlook was somewhat heavy and sour; but when he did smile, it was his sire the sun, bursting out of a black cloud. There was a sudden flash of intelligence, wit, and good humour, beaming in his countenance, which I hardly saw in any other." This intelligence was no doubt influenced by his worldliness, as Handel was somewhat of a globetrotter. (It has been said that Handel could insult a person in as many as five different languages, including his native German, which heavily accented his English.)

Because of his unmatched skill at the organ and his tendency to travel, Handel received many job offers from the respected courts of the day. However, he was not particularly intrigued by most of them. Handel was staunchly independent, and his self-assuredness, talent, and business savvy allowed him to set his own working conditions. This self-sufficiency was not at all common for the time.

Despite the fuzzy account of Handel's early life, we can be certain about his love for Italian opera. The composer who popularized the art form of musical drama in England grew up in late seventeenth-century Saxony, Germany. There, at the age of twelve, he signed a eulogy poem for his father, as quoted by biographer Paul Henry Lang, "Georg Friederich Händel, dedicated to the liberal arts."

This story of Handel begins there, in Saxony, with the great composer as just a boy.

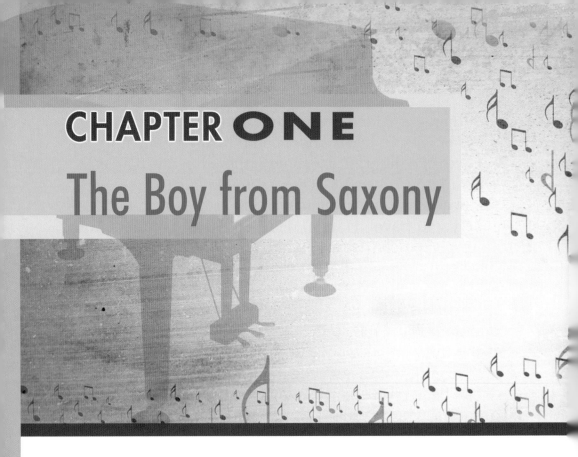

CHAPTER ONE

The Boy from Saxony

Handel's late seventeenth-century Germany was marked by a period of postwar transition, following the Thirty Years' War (1618–1648). This was a series of central European battles fought for various reasons, beginning with religious tension between Protestants and Catholics. Before the war, Germany did not exist as the unified country that it is today. It was a region divided into petty dukedoms and principalities, including Saxony, where Handel was born in the city of Halle. Power over these German territories was held by numerous rulers with varying religious persuasions. Other European nations of the time, including Spain, France, Denmark, and Sweden, were also interested in the German land.

This late seventeenth-century engraving shows a view of Halle, Saxony (modern-day Germany), as it would have looked when Handel was born.

These conflicting interests led from one battle to another, until, in 1648, the Peace of Westphalia ended the war, unifying Germany's divided territories. All of this took place well before Handel's birth in 1685. Halle, however, still bore the war's devastating effects.

HALLE

Halle, a city in the Länder, or state, of Saxony, lies 100 miles (161 kilometers) southwest of Berlin, east of Eisenach, and on the Saale River. The city, named after the Celtic word for salt—the source of its wealth and industry—was also rich in music. Halle was home to a court of many musicians, including organist and composer Samuel

Baroque

Handel began composing toward the end of the baroque period of what is generically referred to as classical music. The French word *baroque* can be traced to the Portuguese word *barroco* and the Spanish word *barrueco*, which are both used to describe an irregularly shaped pearl. Before it was used to describe the style and movement of architecture, art, and music, "baroque" was used negatively to mean "absurd," "grotesque," or "extravagant." In the nineteenth century, after the baroque movement had gradually transitioned to the classical movement, the term was used as we now use it—in reference to the artistic movement of the seventeenth and eighteenth centuries.

Baroque music is generally classified as European classical music from 1600 to 1750. Music from this time is characterized by monody, counterpoint, and emphasis on emotion. In addition to Handel, other well-known baroque composers include Claudio Monteverdi (1567–1643), Henry Purcell (ca. 1659–1695), Johann Sebastian Bach (1685–1750), Domenico Scarlatti (1685–1757), and Antonio Vivaldi (1678–1741).

Scheidt (1587–1654), a native of Halle; English composer William Brade (1560–1630); and German composer Michael Praetorius (1571–1621).

In 1625, in the midst of the Thirty Years' War, Halle was occupied by Albrecht von Wallenstein (1583–1634), commanding general for the army of Holy Roman Emperor Ferdinand II (1578–1637). The court fell apart as a result. Another Saxon court was established in 1638, under Duke August of Saxony. In accordance with the terms of the Peace of Westphalia, it, too, was dismantled. These terms stated that Halle would come under the control of Brandenburg-Prussia, a state of the Roman Empire, upon the Duke of Saxony's death. When the duke died in

1680, Halle's court was moved to and reestablished in Weissenfels.

Early Life

Georg Friederich Händel, who later anglicized his name to George Frideric Handel upon gaining British citizenship, was born on February 23, 1685, in Halle, Germany. He was the second son to his parents (the first died in childbirth), and an elder brother to two sisters, Dorothea Sophia and Johanna Christiana.

The Händel family came from a line of tradespeople. Handel's father, also named Georg, was the son of a coppersmith and was employed as a barber-surgeon, a common joint profession at the time. His mother, Dorothea Taust, was a pastor's daughter and his father's second wife. From these beginnings, Handel's first interest in music is difficult to trace and verify, as is much information about his early years. We know, however, that he somehow learned to play the organ. There are stories that tell of how Handel practiced on a clavichord hidden in the attic because his father did not approve of his musical tendencies. There is no proof for any of them.

There is also no inarguable proof of Handel's early schooling, but evidence suggests that he attended the Gymnasium in Halle. Halle's Gymnasium, a sort of secondary or grammar school, was a Lutheran institution where students were educated in several subjects, including religious studies, Latin, writing, mathematics, and German. Music was not a part of the curriculum. The rector, or head teacher, however, was Johann Praetorius, a talented composer who supported the production of musical plays at the school. Praetorius was also an acquaintance of Handel's father, who had himself attended the Gymnasium. It is safe to guess, then, that Handel also attended the Gymnasium as a youngster, and that, in addition to his studies there, he received his mysterious and undocumented introduction to music and, perhaps, organ playing.

FRIEDRICH WILHELM ZACHOW

Less certain details about Handel's life are accompanied by verified bits of history. One such account is that young Handel traveled with his father to the court at Weissenfels, 20 miles (32 km) south of Halle, where the elder Händel held a court surgeon position to Duke Johann Adolf. (In some versions, the trip was to the court where Handel's half-brother Karl, a son from his father's first marriage, was employed.) The duke happened to pass by as Handel was playing the organ and was so impressed by the youngster, who was between seven and eleven years old, that he urged the boy's father to allow his son to take music lessons.

The elder Händel has been widely described as being strongly opposed to music, instead wanting his son to pursue a career in law. The duke's word, then, must have been quite persuasive. Following the trip to Weissenfels, Handel began taking music lessons from Friedrich Wilhelm Zachow (1663–1712), the organist and director of music at the family's Lutheran church. These lessons gave Handel access to Zachow's extensive library of music, which he frequently browsed. Handel also gained a strong musical foundation. According to John Mainwaring (ca. 1724–1807), who published Handel's biography a year after the composer's death, as quoted by biographer Hogwood, "The first object of [Zachow's] attention was to ground [Handel] thoroughly in the principles of harmony. His next care was to cultivate his imagination, and form his taste." Indeed, Handel's tastes swayed under Zachow's instruction, during which Handel became so skilled at playing the organ that he sometimes substituted for Zachow. Zachow's library fed Handel's curiosity and opened to him a world of music that ranged far in style, technique, and countries of origin.

TRAVELS TO BERLIN

Sometime between 1698 and 1702, Handel made at least one trip to Berlin with Zachow. The exact dates and circumstances of the trip, or trips, are uncertain. However, it was a crucial event in Handel's formative years. In Berlin, Handel had his first up-close exposure to Italian music. While in the Prussian capital, Handel met Italian composers Attilio Ariosti (1666–ca. 1740) and Giovanni Bononcini (1670–1747), who would reappear as a rival later in Handel's musical career.

Handel was, by this time, somewhat well known. In Berlin, Friedrich III, the elector of Brandenburg, who became King Friedrich I of Prussia in 1701, frequently called upon Handel. Impressed by Handel's musical abilities, the elector intended to send the young musician to Italy to develop his talents, then hire Handel for his court. For a musician this young—Handel was a mere teenager—such a court appointment was an honor. But it also involved some risks. Hogwood quotes Mainwaring's explanation that ". . . if [Handel] once engag'd in the King's service, he must remain in it, whether he liked it, or not; and that if he happened to displease, his ruin would be the certain consequence. To accept an offer of this nature was the same thing as to enter into a formal engagement." With the advice of friends and family, Handel declined the offer and began his studies in Halle. This refusal to work in the Berlin court was not the last of Handel's decisions of this nature.

THE UNIVERSITY OF HALLE

Halle itself had no court, but its elector was a great patron of the arts, and immigration into the city was high. This diverse influx of bright minds led to a positive outcome—the founding of the University of Halle in 1694. According to biographer Donald Burrows, the university "quickly gained a reputation for 'progressive' thinking on theology, philosophy and law, involving a rejection of the old 'scholastic' methods and an encouragement of tolerance and freedom of thought." It was in this continually evolving city that Handel grew up, and into this "progressive" university that Handel enrolled as a student in 1702. Despite his interest in the liberal arts, specifically music, Handel decided to study law to respect the wishes of his father, who had died in 1697. At this time, studies in law were not as we think of them today. They were, instead, studies more related to philosophy. Handel's law professors were liberal thinkers who schooled him in Enlightenment ideas and influenced how he thought of himself in relation to society. By the time Handel had finished his studies, he had grown into an independent and self-sufficient man, characteristics that would influence later career choices. All the while, when he was not studying law, he continued studying with Zachow, slowly building upon his reputation as a talented organist.

THEN TO HAMBURG

Just after Handel enrolled at the university, the cathedral of Halle offered him a position as organist. After a year's probation in the position, Handel was permanently offered the respected job, but he declined, as he did before in Berlin. These early career decisions lay the foundations for his future as an independent artist. Handel turned down some honorable proposals, which surely would have puzzled his German contemporaries. His choices, though, would have made complete sense to the traveling Italians he met while in Berlin. They would be true to his wandering nature as well.

With the curiosity and independence he acquired from his studies with Zachow and after his brief enrollment at the University of Halle, Handel decided to move to Hamburg in 1703. The reasons for his choice are clear. Hamburg was a wealthy city that enjoyed a degree of political freedom from the Roman Empire and had been relatively untouched by the Thirty Years' War. It was also home to some of Germany's finest organs—as well as some of the country's most talented organists—and early German opera. Opera in Hamburg was unique to the city. As Lang describes it:

> *The religious subjects were supplanted by worldly ones, the literary quality of the librettos, primitive before, now became coarse, often violating the standards of decency, while the rhymes in the lyrics defy description. Beheadings, with amply flowing artificial blood, were particularly popular, and live animals, even camels and monkeys, appeared to the delight of the audience.*

This daring form of opera would have appealed to Handel, who was rather private about his religion, as he was about most things. In this musically rich and stereotypically baroque setting, Handel began working as a violinist for the opera house orchestra and befriended the twenty-two-year-old Johann Mattheson (1681–1764), to whom Handel would remain close for many years. According to Lang, "Mattheson was a man thoroughly versed in the classics as well as in French and English literature and philosophy, an experienced diplomat, a fine all-round musician—composer, singer, conductor, and player . . . Mattheson was the first thoroughly 'modern' musician Handel got to know and know intimately." There is little doubt that Mattheson strongly influenced Handel's future move to England. He introduced Handel to opera and to John Wyche, an English ambassador whose son, Cyril, Handel would later give harpsichord lessons to. Wyche, in turn, introduced Handel into higher social circles, where Handel acquired even more students.

It was also in Hamburg that Handel became familiar with the music of Reinhard Keiser (1674–1739), a leading composer of early German opera who created more than a hundred operas. Impressed by Keiser's music, Handel soon wrote his own opera, *Almira* (1704). The libretto was both in German and Italian (Handel would come to be fluent in not only these languages, but also English, French, and Latin). *Almira* was elementary in style but quite successful. It ran for about twenty nights, and the positive reception to his first opera set Handel to work on yet another one, *Nero* (1705), which flopped. After three performances, it was never seen or heard again.

At around this time, Handel's friendship with Mattheson became tense. During a performance of

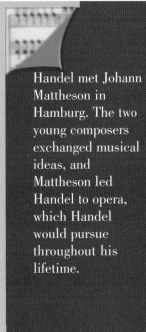

Handel met Johann Mattheson in Hamburg. The two young composers exchanged musical ideas, and Mattheson led Handel to opera, which Handel would pursue throughout his lifetime.

Mattheson's opera *Cleopatra*, Mattheson asked Handel to step down from his seat at the harpsichord. This being Mattheson's opera, Handel should have obliged the wishes of the composer. Handel, however, refused, and the friends were soon engaged in an altercation involving swords. As Mattheson wrote in his biography of German composers, *Musikalische Ehrenpforte* (Musical Gateway of Honor; 1740), as quoted by Lang, "The duel might have ended badly for us both . . . if by God's mercy my sword had not broken on a metal button of my adversary's coat." The two friends reconciled soon after and remained friends for the rest of their lives, though only through letters. Because Keiser dominated Hamburg's opera scene, Handel left for Italy in 1706. He and Mattheson never saw each other again.

CHAPTER **TWO**

A Taste of Italy

Nothing could have prepared the young Saxon for the exciting innovations that were happening in Italy when he arrived there in 1706. Handel's stay was short, but it is difficult to argue that any other time of his life was more influential to his career than his years in Italy.

Italy, in fact, was a major influence on Western music in general. The baroque movement that began there was specifically important to Western musical forms—the song, in particular, as we recognize it today. During the baroque period, the relationship between words and music changed greatly as composers of the time attempted to use music to enrich the sentiments and emotions of spoken words. This eventually led to the creation of opera.

Shown here is a sketch of the stage design for the Italian opera *Giunio Bruto* by Alessandro Scarlatti. Baroque opera sets were elaborate and fancy.

A BRIEF HISTORY OF OPERA

Opera, short for *opera in musica* (work in music), is a form of dramatic entertainment that is performed by singers accompanied by an orchestra. It typically involves music, written by a composer, and words, written by a librettist, which are collected as the libretto (Italian for "little book"). Opera originated in Italy more than 100 years before Handel's arrival. At the time, culture was deeply rooted in the Renaissance movement, which began in northern Italy (Florence is widely accepted as the birthplace) around the thirteenth century, and spread throughout the rest of Europe until roughly the sixteenth century. This movement was characterized by the "rebirth" (the literal meaning of the French word "renaissance" from the Italian *rinascimento*) of classical learning through ancient texts. Applying these texts to mathematics, science, art, and music, among other subjects, led to a revitalized European culture.

During the late period of this movement, in the 1580s, critic, playwright, poet, and composer Giovanni de Bardi (1534–1612) began hosting a gathering of noblemen and musicians, known as the Camerata, to discuss music and the arts. The Camerata allegedly criticized contemporary music for involving too many voices and melodies. This style, known as polyphony, was marked by two or more independent melodies working together in harmony; it was, for some listeners, too complicated. Music historians don't agree on the intellectuals behind opera's precise origins, but whether it was the Camerata or a more informal council of artists around the same time, an alternative to the supposed corruption of music was sought after. The group wished to revive the conventions of ancient Greek drama in order to create a new mode of expression.

Historian and ancient Greek scholar Girolamo Mei (1519–1594), a Camerata member, believed that Greek dramas were originally sung in a single line with only a simple accompaniment. Mei's belief, which today remains unproven, inspired like-minded musicians to return to those traditions while finding a new approach to music that would more effectively enhance and complement the sentiments and emotions the dramas attempted to convey.

These discussions about music eventually led to the creation of *Dafne*, first performed in Florence in 1598, the first piece to be recognized as an opera and which now only survives in fragments. *Dafne's* music was composed by Jacopo Peri (1561–1633), and the text was a poem by Ottavio Rinuccini (1562–1621); both men were Camerata members. *Euridice*, from 1600, also composed and written by Peri and Rinuccini, is the first whole opera that survives. In the book *Baroque Music*, Nicholas Anderson writes, "*Euridice* became a model for composers." That Peri set the standard is no surprise because he thoroughly understood the advantages of this new form. Peri himself explains, as quoted by Anderson:

> *In our speech we intone certain syllables in such a way that harmony can be built upon them, and in the course of speaking we pass through many that are not so intoned until we reach another that permits a movement to a new consonance. Keeping in mind those manners and accents that serve us in our grief and joy, and similar states, I made the bass move in time with these, faster or slower according to the affectations. I held it fixed through both dissonances and consonances, until the voice of the speaker, having run through various notes, arrived at a syllable that, being intoned in ordinary speech, opened the way to a new harmony.*

Other composers of the time must have been thinking along the same lines. The opera form quickly caught on, and the new century ushered in a new era of music. In 1607, Italian composer Claudio Monteverdi's *La favola d'Orfeo* (The Fable of Orpheus) was performed at the annual carnival of Mantua to an enthusiastic and appreciative crowd. *Orfeo* was distinctively divided into parts, like acts of a play, and featured a larger orchestra than had ever been used before. It is close in style to what we recognize as an opera today. Monteverdi soon became a busy and successful composer of opera, following *Orfeo* with equally successful pieces.

By 1637, the first public opera house, the Teatro di San Cassiano in Venice, had opened, bringing opera out of royal courts and into general audiences. This was a huge step forward for the spread of opera, as well as for the spread of art and culture. Opera was no longer exclusively for the ruling class, who had previously held control of the theaters. Patronage of the theater and its composers and musicians was now in the hands of the aristocracy and the merchant class, and opera became available to everyone but the most poor.

As Venetian opera developed and became accessible to all, opera spread throughout Italy, and other European cities were soon falling under its spell. It had already reached Salzburg, in what is now Austria, as early as 1618. Hamburg, where Handel had moved to in 1703, became an important opera center. By 1678, Gerhard Schott (1641–1702), organist Johann Adam Reincken (1623–1722), and Johann Theile (1646–1724) had built Germany's own opera house, Hamburgische Staatsoper (Hamburg State Opera), the first public opera house opened outside Italy. In England, Henry Purcell busied himself with establishing opera there, eventually writing the opera masterpiece *Dido and Aeneas* (1689). The country would not see another composer of operas until the arrival of a young Saxon named Handel.

STUDYING OPERA AT THE SOURCE

As with Handel's early life, not much is known for sure about his brief time in Italy. But it is certain that he was exposed firsthand to Italian opera, and that he met many skilled musicians and influential patrons.

Handel arrived in Florence, Italy, in August 1706, aged twenty-one, probably at the invitation of the prince of Tuscany, Gian Gastone de' Medici (1671–1737). The exact circumstances of his arrival are unknown, except that he paid for the trip himself. There is much to suggest that he refused the allowance offered to him by de' Medici, which corroborates all accounts that Handel was fiercely independent. There is also evidence that Handel did not travel Italy on the cheap. In an article on Handel's time in Italy, Carlo Vitali writes, "The Ruspoli family, his principal hosts in Rome, show that he consumed—presumably not by himself—a truly enormous quantity of victuals [food]." It is widely known that Handel's physique was not slight, and the composer was a great drinker of port.

FIRST PATRONS

In 1707, Handel traveled to Rome, where he gained quick entry into the graces of notable Italian families. According to Lang, "All [Handel] had to do was to go to a church and play the organ, and he became known." And so it was that Handel came to work under his first patrons, important Catholic Church figures, including Cardinals Giovanni Paolo Colonna (1637–1695) and Pietro Ottoboni (1667–1740), for whom he composed cantatas, which are medium-length narrative or descriptive pieces with vocal solos and a chorus or orchestra. At the time, opera had been prohibited in Rome as a result of the Counter-Reformation. This religious movement of the late sixteenth century sought to reaffirm the teachings of the Catholic Church and rid the church of corruption. Opera, viewed as a worldly indulgence, was one such corruption.

Handel often entertained patrons and their guests, as shown above, with his mastery of the keyboard. His musical skill impressed fellow composers and won him many fans.

To escape the religious pressures of such patrons—Handel held on to his Lutheran faith—he came to work for the secular Marquess Francesco Maria Ruspoli, also composing cantatas. During his stay in Italy, Handel composed some 100 cantatas.

DOMENICO SCARLATTI

In addition to making important ties to influential patrons of music, Handel met important contemporary composers, including Domenico Scarlatti, whom he met around 1709, toward the end of his stay in Italy. Scarlatti, son of composer Alessandro Scarlatti (1660–1725), whom Handel also met, was as well known for his skill at the harpsichord as Handel was for his skill at the organ. In keeping with the custom of the time, the meeting of the two composers at the home of Cardinal Ottoboni was marked by duels on the organ and the harpsichord. At the end of the competition, Scarlatti was seen as superior at the harpsichord (some accounts say it was a tie). Handel was unquestionably ruled champion of the organ.

A Hand at Italian Opera

The Catholic Church did not approve of opera, but that did not stop Handel from composing *Rodrigo* in 1707. Handel's first Italian opera premiered in Florence. *Rodrigo* was not Handel's finest, but it was well received, and pieces from it were soon heard in London.

In 1709, Handel composed *Agrippina*, which borrowed from earlier material (as was the tradition), with some help from his friend Mattheson. At its premiere in Venice, as reported by Mainwaring in Hogwood's biography,

> *The audience was so enchanted with this perform-ance . . . The theatre, at almost every pause, resounded with shouts and acclamations of* viva il caro Sassone! *[long live the dear Saxon!] and other expressions of approbation too extravagant to be mentioned. They were thunderstruck with the grandeur and sublimity of his [style]: for never had they known till then all the powers of harmony and modulation so closely arrayed, and so forcibly combined.*

Agrippina ran, to this public reaction, for twenty-seven nights. And with this success under his belt, Handel returned to Germany.

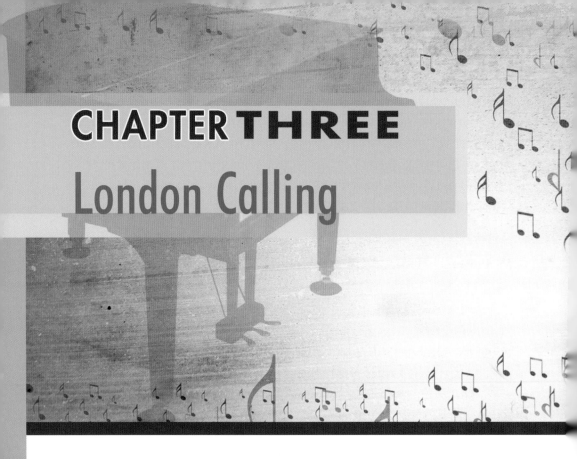

CHAPTER THREE
London Calling

The beloved Saxon found an adoring audience in Italy. Nevertheless, he left and returned to Germany. Religious restrictions in Italy at the time could have sent Handel searching for a more secular environment in which to compose his music. Or the death of his sister, Johanna Christiana, in July 1709, could have brought the young composer's thoughts back to his family in Halle. Whatever his motives were, Handel left the home of opera for Germany, but he wouldn't stay long.

No sooner had Handel arrived in Hanover than he was appointed, on June 15, 1710, kapellmeister, or choir master, for the elector of Hanover, Georg Ludvig (1660–1727), with an annual salary of 1,000 thaler. This would have been a respected and ideal position for any twenty-five-year-old.

For Handel, it would eventually prove not to be enough. A glance at Hanover at the time quickly reveals its appeal, however, even for the fiercely independent Handel.

The first recorded opera in Hanover was performed in 1672. By 1688, Elector Ernst Augustus had ordered the construction of a large theater that was considered one of the finest in Germany. The first opera performed there was by Italian composer Agostino Steffani (1654–1728), who had composed at least eight operas by the time of Handel's arrival. By 1710, there was no active opera company, but Hanover was still a city of talented musicians and singers and other music supporters who would become friends to Handel, including Caroline (1683–1737), the daughter-in-law to Elector Ernst Augustus and future queen of England.

Despite these draws, Handel had already been making plans to leave. As part of the conditions set in his contract with Georg Ludvig, Handel was allowed to leave for considerable lengths of time. A year's absence from Hanover was not only permitted by the elector, but expected. From the terms Handel outlined, anyone could see that the young composer had no intentions of staying put. This time in Hanover would barely last through the end of the year.

THE LURE OF LONDON

Handel made brief stopovers in Düsseldorf to visit the elector of Palatine, and in Halle to visit his mother and pay respects to Johanna Christiana. He would also, for the last time, see Zachow, who died on August 7, 1712. By October or November 1710, Handel was in London. Stories abound as to why Handel made this seemingly sudden trip to London. One is that he was invited by the

Earl of Manchester. Another claims that it was not the earl who invited him, but John Wyche, the English diplomat in Hamburg who was a fan of Handel's, and whose son Handel had tutored. Yet another account suggests that there was no invitation extended at all, and that perhaps Handel was simply prone to travel. Still another indicates that Handel's old friend Johann Mattheson, who was well acquainted with England, may have planted the seeds. Whatever his reasons for leaving Hanover, it is not difficult to see why Handel chose to go to London.

In 1710, London was, as described by Lang, "a great metropolis, the hub of an empire, almost entirely rebuilt after the Great Fire of 1666, and distinguished by many stately public edifices and aristocratic mansions." The city was also experiencing some political change, similar to Handel's home city of Halle at the time of his birth, rebuilding itself through the aftermath of the Glorious Revolution (1688–1689) that involved the overthrow of King James II. More important to Handel, though, was that England was the place to be for artists. In his case, in particular, it was the setting of choice for a composer.

With only a slippery grasp of the English language, Handel waded through the still unstable political environment of England. He evidently did a pretty good job of it, too, because he managed, as a foreigner, to establish his presence among London's elite, the section of society that attended the theater. Handel's acceptance into London's cultured society was a pretty big deal. The city was filled with, as described by Harold C. Schonburg, "a collection of wits, litterateurs, eccentrics, dandies, perverts, poets, essayists, politicians, and courtiers that made [London] one of the great intellectual centers of Europe." This collection included satirist Jonathan Swift (1667–1745) and leader of

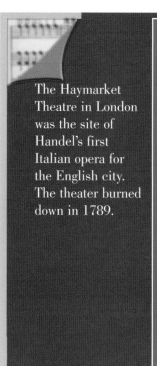

The Haymarket Theatre in London was the site of Handel's first Italian opera for the English city. The theater burned down in 1789.

the scientific revolution, Sir Isaac Newton (1642–1727). In other words, it was not the easiest crowd to impress.

One thing London's inhabitants quickly took to, though, was the Italian-imported opera (at first, anyway, as we shall see). Handel's success in the city, then, is not a complete mystery. On February 24, 1711, his first Italian opera for London, *Rinaldo*, premiered at the Haymarket Theatre. *Rinaldo* was also the first Italian opera composed specifically for the city (previous operas had been borrowed from Italian operas and were bilingual or completely translated into English), and it was met with unanimous approval.

The opera's story was based upon an epic poem by Torquato Tasso (1544–1595) called *Gerusalemme Liberata* (Jerusalem Delivered). It was an embellished account of the First Crusade featuring an enchantress and magic spells. Joseph Addison, a writer for the *Spectator* newspaper,

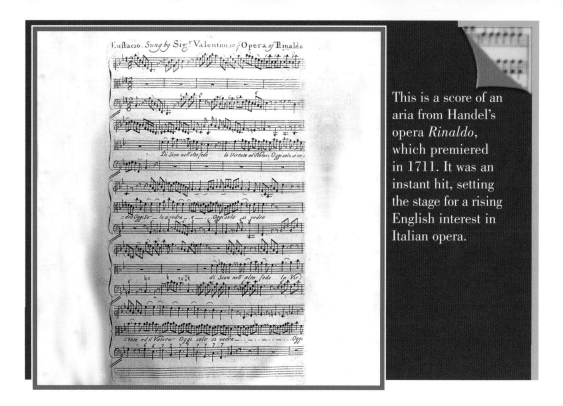

This is a score of an aria from Handel's opera *Rinaldo*, which premiered in 1711. It was an instant hit, setting the stage for a rising English interest in Italian opera.

commented in a March 6, 1711, issue, as quoted by Suzanne Aspden, "The opera houses production of *Rinaldo* is filled with thunder and lightning, illuminations and fire-works; which the audience may look upon without catching cold, and indeed without much danger of being burnt; for there are several engines filled with water, and ready to play at a minute's warning." It was a truly baroque opera.

Whether the audience was in awe of the spectacle *Rinaldo* must have been or was impressed by the music—or both—*Rinaldo* was performed fifteen more times until the close of the opera season in June. (It would be performed fifty-three times in Handel's lifetime, more than any other opera he wrote.) London was sold on Handel, and vice versa. Handel was still employed in Hanover, however, so back he went, with the applause of London still ringing in his ears.

ANOTHER SHORT STAY

On his way back to Hanover, Handel stopped in Düsseldorf again, this time to advise the elector of Palatine on some instruments, and was later back in Halle to visit family, including his new niece, Johanna Friederike Michaelsen, the second child of his sister Dorothea Sophia. But this stay in Hanover would not last much longer than the first. The draw of London was too much for Hanover to compete against, especially because Hanover had no opera house. With the success of *Rinaldo*, Handel was assured a place in England as the country's foremost composer of operas.

Barely a year after Handel had been back in Hanover, composing pieces for his friend the princess Caroline, he again asked the elector for permission to go to England. He promised the elector he would return in a reasonable time. As it turns out, Handel would not return at all.

SETTING THE STAGE

As stated earlier, England was not ignorant of opera before Handel arrived on the scene. Before *Rinaldo*'s exciting run, two theaters in London had been competing with each other to produce operas for the public. That there was a market at all for these theaters to exist shows that the English were open and receptive to this new Italian dramatic form. In January 1705, the Drury Lane Theatre presented *Arsinoe, Queen of Cyprus*, composed mostly by Thomas Clayton, for which all parts were performed in English, and only some of them were sung. It wasn't a huge success, but theatergoers liked it well enough to keep the quasi-opera running for thirty-six shows. Shortly after, the Queen's Theatre was opened in the Haymarket, not showing its first true opera, *Almahide*, until January 1710. (The Queen's Theatre was subsequently named the King's Theatre, based on the monarch's gender, and referred to as the Haymarket Theatre, for the street on which it stood.) *Almahide*, unlike *Arsinoe*, was completely in Italian and sung by Italian singers—the first of its kind to be performed in England.

For the English, the Italian singers were part of the draw. Famous to the time were the Italian castrati, or castrated male singers. The arrival of castrato Nicolo "Nicolini" Grimaldi in London helped pique the interest of opera skeptics. Richard Steele described Nicolini in a December 1708 issue of the *Spectator*, as noted by Christopher Hogwood, "Every limb and every finger contributes to the part he acts . . . inasmuch that a deaf man may go along with him in the sense of it . . . He performs the most ordinary action in a manner suitable to the greatness of character." Nicolini's appearances at the Queen's Theatre helped build a steady following.

The Haymarket Theatre was further strengthened by manager Aaron Hill (1685–1750), who would design the sets for *Rinaldo*, and by assistance from John Jacob Heidegger (1666–1749), a Swiss businessman who knew the theater well. Heidegger's knowledge would prove worthwhile, as, according to Lang, he would "lose no time in associating himself with the coming monarch of opera in London." After the *Rinaldo* performances, the Haymarket Theatre knocked the Drury Lane Theatre out of the running in the competition to establish a scene for Italian opera in England. The Haymarket Theatre became London's principal opera house, and Handel's return would secure that spot.

CHAPTER FOUR

England's Opera Monarch

In the fall of 1712, Handel returned to London, with an improved grasp of the English language since his last visit. He quickly picked up where he had left off when he departed the city just more than a year before. Not too much time had passed since *Rinaldo*'s premiere, so England was ready for more.

Beyond wanting to create more operas with the same success as *Rinaldo* and perhaps to establish connections with would-be patrons, Handel's intentions in England are unknown. When he returned to London, did he intend to stay there, despite the vow he made to the elector of Hanover to go back to Hanover within a reasonable amount of time? If so, the political changes would wind up working in his favor.

NEW PATRONS

Handel supplied eager English audiences with his second opera, *Il Pastor Fido* (The Faithful Shepherd), which premiered on November 22, 1712, at the Haymarket Theatre. It lacked the pomp of *Rinaldo*, and after just six performances, Handel returned to the drawing board and composed the five-act *Teseo* (Theseus) by December 19, for a January 1713 premiere met much greater success. With the mythological Greek sorceress Medea as a leading character, this tragic opera undoubtedly offered dramatic excitement equal to *Rinaldo*. The audience's favor could be measured by the number of seats sold—the theater was full.

On the second night of *Teseo*'s run, the theater manager, Owen Swiney, who had taken over for Aaron Hill, ran off to Italy with the opera's earnings so far. The unpaid cast and crew went on regardless, likely assured that the remaining eleven performances would sell equally well. Swiney was replaced by John Jacob Heidegger, who would manage opera for the next thirty years.

The audience's response to *Teseo* meant more than ticket sales. Its libretto, written by Italian violinist Nicola Francesco Haym (1678–1729), who would serve as librettist to Handel many times, was dedicated to nineteen-year-old Richard Boyle, Earl of Burlington, who offered his home to the composer. Boyle became Handel's patron in 1712, though he was not Handel's first patron in England. (He was previously taken in by one Mr. Andrews, of whom not much is known besides his surname and the fact that he was a wealthy amateur musician.)

A place in the Burlington house was a big deal, as Countess Julianna, the earl's mother, hosted guests

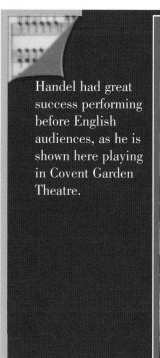

Handel had great success performing before English audiences, as he is shown here playing in Covent Garden Theatre.

including architects, painters, and such noted writers as the English poets Alexander Pope (1688–1744) and John Gay (1685–1732), whom Handel would encounter again later. There was also Dr. John Arbuthnot, a royal physician who would help put the composer in touch with Queen Anne. In agreement with his independent nature, Handel's Burlington hosts gave him free rein to compose as he pleased. He gladly participated in dining and drawing room gatherings, where he was surrounded by the company of leading artists of his time.

Not long after Handel gained patronage from the Earl of Burlington, he, with some aid from Dr. Arbuthnot, captured the attention of Queen Anne, for whom he composed a birthday ode entitled *Eternal Source of Light Divine* in 1713. It was only a matter of time before the queen granted Handel an annual pension of £200. With the aristocratic and royal support of the Earl of Burlington and Queen Anne, Handel, though technically still employed in Hanover, had now very much become a composer for England.

WELCOME BACK THE ELECTOR

Queen Anne reigned until her death in 1714. Her death ended the House of Stuart's control over England and ushered in the rule of the House of Hanover, which was headed by none other than Queen Anne's distant cousin Georg Ludvig, the elector of Hanover—and Handel's employer. With the Hanover succession, Georg Ludvig was crowned King George I of England in September 1714.

If King George was angry that Handel had taken an extended leave from his Hanover post, there were no signs of it. In the years since Handel left Hanover, he had firmly established himself as England's very own opera composer, so the former elector wouldn't have been completely surprised to see Handel again. George I added another £200 per year to the lifelong pension that Handel had received from Queen Anne for a total of £400 (approximately $79,000 today).

ENCORE!

The Haymarket Theatre revived *Rinaldo* in January 1715, with castrato Nicolini back in the leading role, and with the royal family in attendance. The audience was apparently pleased with Nicolini's return, for, according to Christopher Hogwood, the theater's managers issued a warning stating, "Whereas by the frequent calling for the songs again Opera have been too tedious, therefore the singers are forbidden to sing any song above once; and it is hoped nobody will call for 'em or take it ill when not obeyed."

Good standing with royalty was nothing to be scoffed at, nor was strong audience support. But for Handel this still was not enough; he would soon seek other means of employment.

THE ROYAL ACADEMY OF MUSIC

In the meantime, opera seasons came and went, and Handel assuredly kept his fans. He also maintained good relations with King George, composing for him the well-known *Water Music* in 1717. The king enjoyed *Water Music* so much that he ordered the piece to be played three times as he sailed on his barge up and down the Thames River. *Water Music* was one of many instrumental pieces Handel composed around this time while still composing operas. Others include the so-called eleven *Chandos Anthems* that Handel composed with the support of yet another patron, James Brydges, the Earl of Carnarvon, who would also later become the Duke of Chandos. Following Handel's employment with the Earl of Burlington, Handel was invited to join the Earl of Carnarvon at his home, Cannons, which reportedly cost around £230,000 (about $46 million today) to build. This was a good patron for Handel to have. He was hired by the earl as composer in residence, working alongside the German composer Johann Christoph Pepusch (1667–1752), who held the post of director of music. Handel would remain in this position until February 20, 1719.

On that day, Handel wrote a letter to his brother-in-law, Michael Michaelsen, widowed husband to his late sister Dorothea Sophia, who had died the month before.

Handel's Love Life

Shown here is a portrait of Queen Anne, one of the many patrons and fans whom Handel found in England.

Biographies of Handel are filled with pages of information relating to his career in composing music and not much else. Of Handel's personal life, there is only speculation about whether he had any romantic relationships with anyone, although there are indications (all unproven) that he had such relationships with some of the women employed to sing in his operas. His biographer Mainwaring, whose information is sometimes unreliable or confused, did shed some light on the matter, and as he was alive during Handel's time, it is likely that some of his knowledge on Handel's love life is true.

There is evidence that Handel might have had a relationship with Lucrenzia D'André, a singer for the court at Florence, Italy. Mainwaring also writes of a possible relationship with Vittoria Tarquini, known as La Bombace, who was also in Florence. Indeed, there are many possibilities. Mainwaring, however, indirectly shed further light on Handel's personal relations. Scribbled in the margin of a copy of his biography on Handel is the note, as recorded by Schonburg, "G. F. Handel scorned the advice of any but the Woman he loved, but his Amours were rather of short duration, and always within the pale of his own profession." The handwriting of the note has been attributed to King George II.

It is not unusual that Handel never married. He was a successful businessman in addition to being a renowned—and quite busy—composer. It was likely well understood that the prolific composer would have chosen his career over a more family-oriented life, although he did provide well for his mother throughout her life, as well as for his sisters and their children, particularly his niece Johanna Friederike Michaelsen, who became the main beneficiary of his estate.

In the letter, he stated his regrets for not being able to come to Halle, for he was being kept in London "by affairs of the greatest moment, on which (I venture to say) all my fortunes depend," as quoted by Christopher Hogwood.

The "greatest moment" to which Handel referred was the founding of the Royal Academy of Music, with John Heidegger as the manager, and Paolo Rolli as the chief poet and librettist. Mainwaring reports, as quoted by Hogwood,

> *a project was formed by the Nobility for erecting an academy at the Haymarket. The intention of this musical Society, was to secure to themselves a constant supply of Opera to be composed by HANDEL, and performed under his direction. For this end a subscription was set on foot: and as his . . . Majesty was pleased to let his name appear at the head of it, the Society was dignified with the title of the Royal Academy.*

The academy was established in April to firmly bring Italian opera to London, with a subscription fee of £200 (about $39,508), with the agreement that subscribers would also be held responsible for additional annual "calls" for more money. By May, there were sixty-three subscribers, some of whom contributed up to £1,000 ($197,540), in addition to the royal grant of £1,000. In exchange for their contributions, academy subscribers were given two tickets to attend the opera for twenty-one years (this was later revised to fourteen years).

It was a shaky system dependent on too many unstable factors including the subscribers themselves, as well as demanding singers. Academy estimates were incredibly inaccurate from the start, and Handel's own salary as the appointed master of the orchestra is unknown. As the result of these drawbacks, the Royal Academy eventually went bankrupt by 1728. Nevertheless, while the academy lasted, its members attempted to run a successful and profitable business. The academy, in spite of financial difficulty, still found its footing and is generally regarded as an artistic achievement.

The First Season

Before the start of the first season, Handel traveled to continental Europe, including a detour to visit family in Halle, to recruit singers. He attempted to bring back castrati, in particular the castrato known as Senesino (Francesco Bernardi; ca. 1690–1750). The Royal Academy's first season, however, opened without Senesino and, instead, with Margarita Durastante, a famous soprano whom Handel had met in his earliest travels to Italy. Durastante was nicknamed the "Elephant" by librettist Rolli, and the name stuck, unfortunately for the academy. As the castrato Nicolini demonstrated earlier, the singers and actors were as important as the opera itself.

The first performance was of Giovanni Porta's *Numitore*. Lack of documentation suggests that it was unremarkable. The second performance, however, of Handel's *Radamisto*, with a libretto by Nicola Haym, stirred up much more excitement. According to Mainwaring, as quoted by Hogwood, "The applause it received was almost as extravagant as his AGRIPPINA had excited: the crowds and tumults of the house at Venice were hardly equal to those at London." The theater was so packed that people wishing to see the opera were turned away at the Haymarket doors. *Radamisto*'s positive reception proved that Handel's music stood tall even without the greatest singers of the day.

Stars of the Opera

These singers, at any rate, would prove to be more trouble than they were worth. They were, after all, part of the reason the Royal Academy failed. The sought-after castrato Senesino eventually arrived at the academy in September 1720, and remained its star until the company's fall eight years later. With a fee that eventually reached £2,000 ($398,025) a year, it's easy to see why the academy eventually could not keep up with its expenses. He also reportedly did not get along with Handel, who was prone to bursts of anger. (During an argument with soprano Francesca Cuzzoni, Handel reportedly threatened to throw her out the window.) There was also the rivalry between Cuzzoni, who was supposedly quite unattractive, and Faustina Bordoni, considerably more accomplished and attractive.

Handel was not the sole composer of operas for the Royal Academy. Along with singers, other composers were also drawn in, including Giovanni Bononcini and Attilio Ariosti, whom Handel had met in Italy. The three composers engaged in composing contests held by the Royal Academy directors. Of the 487 performances given by the Royal Academy at the Haymarket Theatre, about half can be credited to Handel.

The Academy's Decline, the End of Opera?

Much happened in the years leading up to the academy's inevitable end: Handel moved into his house at 25 Brook

Street in 1723, where he would live until he died; he was appointed master of music to the princesses Anne and Caroline in 1724; he officially became a British citizen in 1727; George I died and was succeeded by King George II also in 1727; and, finally, John Gay and Johann Pepusch's *Beggar's Opera* was performed sixty-two times—a record for the time—to adoring crowds, premiering on January 29, 1728. Even with the performances of many of Handel's finest operas, including *Giulio Cesare in Egitto* (Julius Caesar in Egypt), the Royal Academy of Music finally announced its closing in June later that year.

THE BEGGAR'S OPERA

The decline of public approval of opera has many causes, but the great success of *The Beggar's Opera* is an obvious marker of England's changing tastes. Featuring a libretto by Gay and music by Pepusch, *The Beggar's Opera* was a lighthearted musical comedy—in English. It was quite a contrast to Handel's opera serias, or "serious operas," and a welcome one at that. Opera serias, which comprise the majority of Handel's operas, were concerned with mytho-logical and classical subjects that eventually grew heavy and dull for theatergoers' tastes. *The Beggar's Opera*, then, was a fresh change. English members of the audience could relate to the play's subjects—British statesman Sir Robert Walpole and famous criminal Jonathan Wild—and understand the humor, since the text was in English.

Italian opera had done well in England, but now, it seemed, the English had a dramatic form of their own.

CHAPTER **FIVE**
Hallelujah!

The success of *The Beggar's Opera* and the failure of the Royal Academy of Music should have persuaded Handel to give up. But for Handel, the collapse of the first Royal Academy only meant that a new one should be formed, without repeating the mistakes of the initial attempt. The academy was bankrupt, but Handel was not, so, in 1729, with John Heidegger at his side, he took over the academy and set off to recruit new singers, presumably ones with more agreeable dispositions.

A LAST ATTEMPT

Travels to Italy by both Handel and Heidegger were not altogether successful. They tried to recruit the famous castrato Farinelli, but with no luck. Also, Handel made yet another trip back to Halle in June 1729, to visit his blind and ailing mother. He must have known this would be his last visit with her (she would die the following year); he spent all his time with her, declining even Johann Sebastian Bach's request to visit him in Leipzig. When Handel and Heidegger returned to London, they had in tow Anna Strada, said to be even more ghastly than Cuzzoni (while soprano Durastante was nicknamed the Elephant, Londoners took to calling Strada the Pig) but with a better voice, and castrato Antonio Bernacchi, among others. Librettist Nicola Haym, who had died in August 1729, was replaced by Giacomo Rossi.

At the end of the year, the second academy's first season opened with *Lotario*, which was a complete failure. The drama was filled with, what one might interpret as signs to come, attempted suicides. It was clear from the opera's subject that Handel had not produced what London theatergoers wanted—that is, something like *The Beggar's Opera*. He followed with *Partenope* on February 30, 1730, to a pleasantly surprised audience. Unlike his previous opera serias, *Partenope* was almost a comedy and featured fresh music.

Pleased as the audience was, though, *Partenope* was not successful. In fact, the first season was almost a complete failure. *The Beggar's Opera* really had changed the public's tastes. It no longer mattered to the English that they had their very own composer of Italian opera. *The Beggar's Opera* showed them that they could have their own musical form in their own language. The remaining days of the second Royal Academy would play out much like the first days, with highs and lows, but still without strong public support. And Handel, like opera, seemed to be falling out of favor as well. Around this uncertain time in Handel's career, Joseph Goupy, a set designer for the academy, began circulating a rather unflattering and insulting cartoon of Handel as a pig seated before an organ. It was quickly passed around London, further affecting Handel's reputation.

The Opera of the Nobility

To further tip the scales against Handel, a rival opera house at Lincoln's Inn Fields, the so-called Opera of the Nobility, was established in 1733. There, Italian composer Nicola Porpora (1686–1768) directed many of Handel's old cast members, including Senesino and Antonio Montagnana, a bass singer Handel had alienated a year or two before, and, later, even Francesca Cuzzoni. As a double blow to Handel, Porpora was also a famous vocal teacher whose students included the even more famous Farinelli, whom Handel had attempted, without success, to recruit for his own theater. Farinelli would join the Opera of the Nobility the following year.

Rivalry between the Opera of the Nobility and the second Royal Academy of Music went on for some time, but Farinelli assured the former's supremacy. Even with the support of King George II (who was giving Handel an annual pension of £1,000 [about $205,411]), Queen Caroline, and Princess Anne, the second academy folded without much ado.

THE TRUE LAST ATTEMPT

The final end to the Royal Academy of Music did not mark the end of Handel's opera career. In 1734, with the folding of the academy, Handel joined theater manager John Rich, formerly of Lincoln's Inn Fields during *The Beggar's Opera*'s days, at the Theatre Royal in Covent Garden. This theater opened on February 19, 1736, with support from George II's son and enemy, Prince Frederick of Wales, premiering *Alexander's Feast* with English actors singing in English. The theater was full, and its audience liked what it heard. It apparently wasn't enough, though. All audiences seemed impossible to please. The Opera of the Nobility, now at the Haymarket Theatre, closed in June 1737, due to bankruptcy, and the Covent Garden Theatre followed two weeks later.

FAILING HEALTH

Even with the bankruptcy of the Covent Garden Theatre, Handel was not without funds. His health, however, was another matter. The rivalry and years of tireless composing had caught up with him, and in April 1737, he reportedly suffered from attacks of rheumatism, or swelling of the joints and muscles, that left him without the use of his right hand. This handicap was temporary and did not stop Handel from composing, but it would return later, and with greater seriousness.

THE FAT LADY SINGS . . .

After journeying to Aachen, Germany (or, as it was commonly referred to by its French name, Aix-la-Chapelle), where he would frequently travel to for treatments for his paralysis, Handel returned once again to London and joined Heidegger and yet another opera company at his old theater at Haymarket. It was not a completely unsuccessful venture, but despite his efforts to keep the English audience's attention, Handel's final opera, *Deidamia* (1740), was met with the same generally unenthusiastic responses. *Deidamia*'s February 1741 performance would mark the final production of an opera under Handel's direction.

Handel was not completely out of England's good graces, however. Music fans may have grown tired of opera, but Handel was still quite adored. In April 1738, a statue of him by sculptor Louis François Roubiliac was erected at Vauxhall Gardens (it has stood, since 1965, at the Victoria & Albert Museum, to which it was sold). This event proves his popularity, as statues are most often made to honor someone after he or she has died. With yet more energy to compose, and an audience still welcoming of the composer, if not his operas, Handel began composing the oratorio that would make his name famous for hundreds of years after his time.

A New Form

The oratorio itself was not a new form. Its origins date to sixteenth-century Rome, to Filippo Neri, who founded a society known as the Congregazione dell'Oratorio (Congregation of the Oratory), from which the oratorio gets its name. Neri's congregations included singing passages from Scriptures, which eventually became what we know as oratorios.

Handel had already tried his hand at writing English oratorios, grand musical works with vocals and an orchestra—sort of like operas but without costumes, scenery, or action, and usually religious in subject. His first English oratorio was *Esther* (1732), which premiered at the Haymarket Theatre and marked the first performance of an

Was Handel a Plagiarist?

By today's standards, and, indeed, by the literal definition of the word, Handel could quite accurately be called a plagiarist, or someone who takes someone else's work and passes it off as his or her own. By the standards of his own days, however, "borrowing" from other composers was not unheard of, and Handel's own practice of it was quite common. In Handel's time, most people were accepting of the liberties he took with other composers' works, and his audiences even expected them. French author Abbé Prévost wrote, as quoted by Harold C. Schonburg, "Some critics . . . accuse him of having borrowed the matter of many beautiful things from [composer Jean-Baptiste] Lully, especially from our French cantatas, which he has the skill, so they say, to disguise in the Italian style. But the crime would be venial [pardonable], were it certain."

Given how prolific Handel was throughout his musical career, one can see how he could have easily been swayed to improvise others' pieces and then claim them as his. Regardless, Handel's plagiarism was recognized in his own day. Composers from whom he borrowed include, Lully (as mentioned), Reinhard Keiser, Karl Heinrich Graun, Francesco Antonio Urio, his rival Giovanni Bononcini, and himself.

oratorio in London. The oratorio he was about to write, however, would, without contest, become his most famous.

In early August 1741, following his last operatic attempt, Handel was invited to go to Dublin, Ireland, by William Cavendish, who was the lord lieutenant of Ireland and the duke of Devonshire, to participate in a season of oratorio concerts for charity organizations. Handel had been persuaded by author Charles Jennens (1700–1773), a longtime fan of Handel's who eventually came to be the composer's librettist, to resume his work with the oratorio. And so, at age fifty-six, Handel began composing music for Jennens's libretto, beginning on

August 22, and finishing just twenty-four days later, on September 14. Upon its completion, Handel is said to have exclaimed, as quoted in Lang's biography, "I did think I did see all Heaven before me and the great God Himself." This oratorio, publicized as "a new sacred Oratorio," was *Messiah*.

HANDEL'S *MESSIAH*

Messiah premiered for a charity concert in Dublin, Ireland, on April 13, 1742. Although it is now associated with Christmas performances, it was originally intended for Lent and Easter, as its first spring performance indicates. The subject of Jennens's libretto was apt for the occasion. It consisted of lines taken straight from the Bible about the salvation, resurrection, and redemption of the Messiah, or "anointed one," Jesus Christ. This overtly religious subject was not typical for Handel, who had previously stuck to secular themes for the majority of his works. *Messiah*, however, was most likely composed specifically for this charity performance.

As the public reception to *Messiah*'s premiere would prove, Handel was still greatly respected. Following the performance, the *Dublin Journal* reported, as quoted in Richard Luckett's *Handel's Messiah: A Celebration*,

> *On Tuesday last [the 13th] Mr. Handel's Sacred Grand Oratorio, the MESSIAH, was performed at the New Musick-Hall in Fishamble-street; the best Judges allowed it to be the most finished piece of Musick. Words are wanting to express the exquisite Delight it afforded to the admiring crouded Audience. The Sublime, the Grand, and the Tender, adapted*

to the most elevated, majestick and moving Words,
conspired to transport and charm the ravished
Heart and Ear.

Approximately 700 people were in attendance, and the proceeds, which amounted to about £400 ($87,688 today), were divided evenly among three charities, "Prisoners, the Charitable Infirmary, and Mercer's Hospital," as named in the *Dublin Journal* article. In Handel's remaining years, he would continue performing acts of philanthropy, especially for the Foundling Hospital in London, which he would play a major role in establishing.

Despite *Messiah*'s success, not everyone was happy with how it had turned out. The librettist, Jennens, was far from pleased. In a letter to his friend Edward Holdsworth in early 1743, Jennens wrote, as quoted by Christopher Hogwood, "His *Messiah* has disappointed me, being set in great hast, tho' he said he would be a year about it, & make it the best of all his Compositions. I shall put no more Sacred Words into his hands, to be thus abus'd." Jennens's discontentment with *Messiah*, though, and his letters to Handel urging him to rewrite parts, are one indication of how *Messiah* came to be altered several times after its original composition, for which there is no existing score.

Beyond *Messiah*

In 1743, back in London, Handel again grew ill, as paralysis of his hand returned. Jennens wrote in another letter, "I hear Handel has a return of his Paralytick Disorder, which affects his Head & Speech." As it did not hinder him before, this did not keep Handel from composing now. He began working on *Semele* and finished in four weeks;

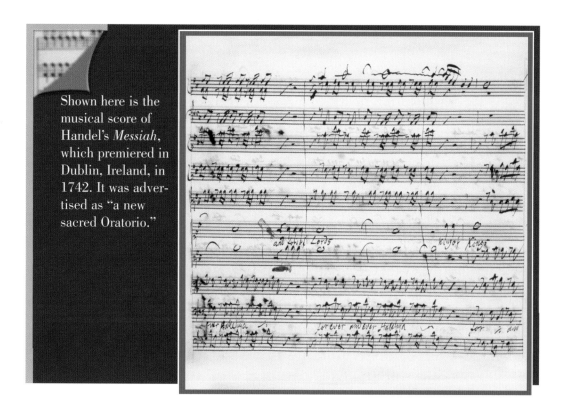

Shown here is the musical score of Handel's *Messiah*, which premiered in Dublin, Ireland, in 1742. It was advertised as "a new sacred Oratorio."

this was only the beginning of Handel's final compositions, including *Music for the Royal Fireworks* (1749), his last commissioned piece for the royal House of Hanover. He would continue composing well over a dozen more new pieces, until 1751, while composing *Jephtha*, when he lost sight in his left eye. (Even then, he still managed to finish composing the oratorio and to give its first performance in 1752.) Handel's blindness did not stop him, either, from playing the organ twice that year in charity concerts at the Foundling Hospital. Multiple surgeries were attempted to restore his sight, but all efforts were unsuccessful.

The Foundling Hospital

In 1742, construction of the Foundling Hospital for underprivileged children began at Lamb's Conduit Fields in London after a royal charter for it was issued in 1739 at the urging of Thomas Coram, a retired sea captain. Beginning in 1749, and for the rest of his life, Handel was active in the upkeep of the hospital, mainly by offering charity concerts for the hospital's cause. That year, a concert in the hospital's unfinished chapel that included selections from *Music for the Royal Fireworks* was given, raising £350 ($73,183 today), plus an additional £2,000 ($418,189 today) from King George II. The following year, Handel was elected governor of the hospital.

THE TWILIGHT YEARS

In addition to the Foundling Hospital, Handel was charitable to himself and those around him. In 1750, the same year Johann Sebastian Bach died following a botched eye surgery, Handel purchased an original painting by famous Dutch painter Rembrandt (1606–1669) for the sum of £8,000 ($1,678,289 today), and drafted a will in which he left the bulk of his wealth and belongings, including his house on Brook Street, to his dear friend and amanuensis from Germany, John Christopher Smith, and his niece Johanna Friederike (he also traveled to Germany for the last time). Shortly after, he lost sight in both eyes, which no surgeries could correct, and in 1753, he made his final public performance at yet another charity concert for the Foundling Hospital. The following year, 1754, marked the final performance of a Handel opera until the twentieth century, and April 14, 1759, marked the end of Handel's life. The composer died at age seventy-four, at his home on Brook Street. On the night before his death, as reported in a letter by his friend James Smyth, according to biographer Hogwood, Handel said "that he had now done with the world."

CHAPTER SIX
Handel's Legacy

The world, however, was not done with Handel. Though he requested a private burial at Westminster Abbey, more than 3,000 people showed up for his funeral. Hogwood writes, "His death was reported widely in the press, many newspapers anticipating the event by a couple of days and almost all emphasizing that he died worth upwards of £20,000 [about $4,040,910 today]." Handel's tomb would be neighbor to, 111 years later, that of English novelist Charles Dickens (1812–1870).

Today, a young artist seeking fame and finding it is not unheard of; this seems to happen every day. It is exceptional, however, when the mark an artist leaves lasts indefinitely. Such is the case with Handel. Johann Sebastian Bach, Handel's baroque contemporary, never left his native Germany, which was a setback in terms of his popularity. As it happens with many artists, Bach did not become world famous until long after his death. Handel, on the other hand, great traveler that he was, brought his music to many and was internationally renowned throughout his lifetime, as well as for centuries after.

None of this success, of course, could have been possible without the talent to back it. Handel's musical genius and self-reliance allowed him to decline the generous offers from all the royal patrons at his heels, and to establish his own scene in England, under his own terms. These qualities, plus an undying passion for music and a drive for ceaselessly composing it also allowed Handel to own the stage for opera and oratorio in a country not his own. This incredible lifetime of achievements makes Handel not only a cultural emblem for England, but a symbol of all baroque music.

Handel left behind more than fifty operas, dozens of oratorios, and hundreds of instrumental works, concerts of which continue to be held. With just these pieces—preserved for centuries after they were written—and only snippets of the life of the man who wrote them, we can still assemble a tremendous portrait of this baroque icon. His influence extends to our time, but it began in the composer's own time. Not long after Handel's death, he was proclaimed by composers Joseph Haydn (1732–1809) and Beethoven to be both a master and the greatest composer who ever lived. Beethoven stated his reverence of Handel on many occasions. In 1824, just three years before his death, Beethoven professed, "I would bare my head and kneel at his grave." On his own deathbed, Beethoven is said to have quoted from *Messiah* itself.

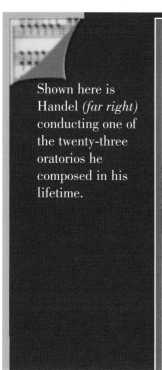

Shown here is Handel *(far right)* conducting one of the twenty-three oratorios he composed in his lifetime.

As we know, the 1742 premiere of Handel's most famous oratorio, *Messiah*, would not even remotely be its last performance. While the popularity of his other compositions has waxed and waned, *Messiah* continues to be as popular as it was when it debuted. Perhaps more than any other musical piece, *Messiah* resonates among the secular and nonsecular alike, beginning in Handel's time and stretching to the present. It moves people in the most sacred settings, such as churches, to the most accessible, including the concert halls of today. Vocal music in Handel's day, after all, was developed to better communicate the emotions the words attempted to convey. Time, customs, and fads aside, no sound will move a crowd more quickly to their feet than Handel's "Hallelujah" chorus. This is Handel's legacy. It exists in the musical marks he left on the world—unchanged by time, and more persistent still than the great composer who left them.

TIMELINE

1685	Georg Friederich Händel is born.
1692	Handel begins taking music lessons from Friedrich Wilhelm Zachow.
1697	Handel's father dies.
1702	Handel enrolls at the University of Halle.
1703	Handel befriends composer Johann Mattheson.
1704	Handel composes his first opera, *Almira*. He and Mattheson fight in a duel.
1706–1710	Handel travels to Italy, the home of opera.
1710	Handel becomes kapellmeister to the elector of Hanover. He composes his first Italian opera, *Rinaldo*.
1717	Handel composes *Water Music*.
1719	The Royal Academy of Music is founded; Handel is appointed master of the orchestra.
1724	Handel is appointed court composer for the Royal Chapel and master of music to Princesses Anne and Caroline.
1728	John Gay and Johann Christoph Pepusch's *Beggar's Opera* premieres.
1732	*Esther* premieres on February 23.
1741	Handel completes *Messiah* in twenty-four days.
1750	Handel is elected governor of the Foundling Hospital.
1751	Handel begins losing his sight.
1759	Handel dies at his home on Brook Street.

LIST OF SELECTED WORKS

OPERAS

Almira (1705)
Nero (1705)
Rodrigo (1707)
Agrippina (1709)
Rinaldo (1711)
Teseo (1712)
Radamisto (1720)
Giulio Cesare in Egitto (1724)
Orlando (1733)
Alcina (1735)
Serse (1738)
Deidamia (1741)

ORATORIOS

La Resurrezione (1708; Italian)
Brockes Passion (1716; German)
Esther (1732; English)
Saul (1736; English)
Israel in Egypt (1739; English and Italian)
Messiah (1742; English)
Samson (1743; English)

Belshazzar (1745; English)
Solomon (1749; English)
Jephtha (1751; English)

ODES

Eternal Source of Light Divine, or *Ode for the Birthday of Queen Anne* (1713; English)
Zadok the Priest (1727)
Alexander's Feast (1736; English)

DRAMAS

Acis and Galatea (1732; Italian and English)
Semele (1744; English)
Hercules (1745; English)

INSTRUMENTAL PIECES

Utrecht Te Deum (1713)
Jubilate (1713)
Water Music (1717)
Chandos Anthems (1718)

GLOSSARY

amanuensis A literary or artistic assistant.

aria From the Italian for "air," a musical piece, usually performed by a singer with orchestral accompaniment, contained within a larger work.

baroque A European classical music movement that spanned from around 1600 to 1750.

counterpoint The art or technique of setting a melody, or melodies, against another.

elector A German prince of the Holy Roman Empire.

Enlightenment A European intellectual movement of the seventeenth and eighteenth centuries that emphasized reason and individualism over tradition.

Glorious Revolution The overthrow of the Catholic king James II of England, who was succeeded by his Protestant daughter, Mary, and her husband, William of Orange.

kapellmeister The leader or conductor of a choir or orchestra.

libretto The text of an opera, from the Italian word meaning "little book."

monody Music that features only one melodic line with an accompanying part.

opera seria Italian for "serious opera." An opera, typically Italian, that has a mythological, classical, or historical theme.

secular Without religious or spiritual basis.

FOR MORE INFORMATION

The American Handel Society
University of Maryland, School of Music
College Park, MD 20742
(909) 607-3568
Web site: http://www.americanhandelsociety.org

The Handel House Museum
25 Brook Street
Mayfair
London, W1K 4HB
England
Web site: http://www.handelhouse.org

The Handel Institute
Barber Institute
The University of Birmingham
Edgbaston, Birmingham B15 2TS
England

WEB SITES

Due to the changing nature of Internet links, Rosen Publishing has developed an online list of Web sites related to the subject of this book. This site is updated regularly. Please use this link to access the list:

http://www.rosenlinks.com/mth/hawo

FOR FURTHER READING

Barber, David W. *Bach, Beethoven and the Boys: Music History as It Ought to Be Taught*. Toronto, Canada: Sound and Vision, 1986.

Barber, David W. *Getting a Handel on the Messiah*. Toronto, Canada: Sound and Vision, 1994.

Thompson, Wendy. *Handel* (Illustrated Lives of the Great Composers). New York, NY: Omnibus Press, 1995.

BIBLIOGRAPHY

Anderson, Nicholas. *Baroque Music: From Monteverdi to Handel*. New York, NY: Thames and Hudson Inc., 1994.

Aspden, Suzanne. "The Rinaldo Story." The Academy of Ancient Music Web site. September 2000. Retrieved February 25, 2005 (http://www.aam.co.uk/index. htm?main%3Efeatures/0010.htm).

Burrows, Donald. *Handel*. New York, NY: Schirmer Books, 1994.

Butt, John. "Germany—Education and Apprenticeship." *The Cambridge Companion to Handel*. Donald Burrows, ed. New York, NY: Cambridge University Press, 1997.

Hogwood, Christopher. *Handel*. New York, NY: Thames and Hudson Inc., 1984.

Lang, Paul Henry. *George Frideric Handel*. Mineola, NY: Dover Publications Inc., 1994.

Leissa, Brad, and David Vickers. "Chronology." GFHandel.org. May 31, 2001. Retrieved June 10, 2005 (http://gfhandel.org).

Luckett, Richard. *Handel's Messiah: A Celebration*. New York, NY: Harcourt, Brace & Company, 1992.

Schonburg, Harold C. *The Lives of the Great Composers*, Third Edition. New York, NY: W. W. Norton & Company, 1997.

Vitali, Carlo. "Italy—Political, Religious and Musical Contexts." *The Cambridge Companion to Handel*. Donald Burrows, ed. New York, NY: Cambridge University Press, 1997.

INDEX

About the Author

Lavina Lee grew up in northern California, where she took piano lessons for thirteen years, and both violin and flute lessons for two. She received her bachelor's degree in English and art history. This is her first book.

Photo Credits

Cover Gerald Coke Handel Collection, Foundling Museum, London/ The Bridgeman Art Library; p. 4 © Mary Evans Picture Library/The Image Works; p. 9 The Art Archive/Handel Museum Halle/Dagli Orti (A); pp. 17, 19 © akg-images; pp. 24, 30, 55 © Lebrecht/The Image Works; p. 29 Guildhall Library, City of London/The Bridgeman Art Library; p. 35 Private Collection/The Bridgeman Art Library; p. 38 © Sotheby's/akg-images; p. 51 © British Library.

Designer: Nelson Sá; **Editor:** Wayne Anderson
Photo Researcher: Amy Feinberg